Business Success Starts With Health

Achieving Health For Business Entrepreneurs

Todd Reinker

Table Of Contents

Introduction

You are the owner of a business; therefore it is crucial that you stay in great physical and mental health. Sure, you may have automated systems and staff members that can take care of your business should need to take a leave of absence, but each time that you fall ill, you eat away at your overall vitality and the passion you hold for your business becomes lackluster. It does not matter what systems you have in place, when you lose your passion, your profits and your business begins to suffer greatly.

In a previous report, time management was discussed as well as your hourly value. If a small business owner is not working in a productive manner, or not working at all, then they are not making money. This is why it is so crucial to improve your health and work hard to maintain it.

We are not just talking about how costly it can be to get sick. Each year, businesses shell out forty five billion dollars in the United States for illness costs, and this does not include your own personal medical expenses or the time you have to take off of work.

It can also be argued that mental health can be even more detrimental to a business if it is in poor shape. For instance, stress can cause you to feel:

- Depressed
- Overwhelmed
- Angry
- Fatigued
- Unable to focus
- Irritable
- Unsure about your success

- Nervous
- Unable to make decisions
- Completely burned out

In addition, stress can cause a number of different illnesses, which we will discuss further in the following chapter. To be frank, the state of your mental well-being is a key factor in the success of your business and also your own happiness. If you are constantly feeling too stressed and overwhelmed, you simply cannot enjoy life. Furthermore, you cannot focus on your business in a positive way and it will become nearly impossible to be productive. If you have been feeling this way, you need to do something and you need to do it quickly.

Remember: You Can Control Your Life, Your Success And Your Health

The goal of this book is to provide you with the right tools, resources, knowledge and power to regain control of your mental and physical health.

By taking these steps to better improve your health, you will not only find great success and more profits, but you will find it much easier to enjoy all of your success as well. A million dollars will do you no good if you are too sick or depressed to actually enjoy it.

This book is separated into five different chapters. Each section will discuss a different component of self-care. This includes learning how to foster better mental health, diet tips, exercise help, sleep and how to live a more meaningful life. Along the way, we will ask you some important questions that are designed to make you take an honest look at your habits and your lifestyle. Every single person in this world could use a little improvement. If you take care of your physical and mental health, they will both take care of you. Let's begin!

Getting Rid Of Stress

Stress and its negative effects are discussed so often that many people simply ignore it whenever the subject is brought up. To be quite honest, most people find stress to be completely unavoidable. It is simply a part of life for them. Furthermore, telling someone to just "reduce stress" is even less productive than telling someone to just "lose weight". It is just not that simple. How can you reduce stress? Is it important to reduce all types of stress, or just some types? What are some tangible steps that you can take towards reducing the amount of stress in your life? Is it even plausible for you to reduce stress?

Why is there so much talk about stress in the first place? What does this have to do with anything?

Stress can cause a number of different mental health issues, including anger, depression and anxiety. Of course, each one of these conditions can be caused by completely separate factors as well, but stress is by far the biggest factor in the state of your mental health.

Let's say that the alarm clock has just gone off on Monday morning. After you get out of bed, you see that your to-do list is about a mile long as you have over a dozen phone calls to return, your email inbox is spilling over, the house you live in is a complete disaster, and to top it all off the postman just left and never delivered the important tax information you needed to file on time. Now you are going to be late with the IRS and you feel like you might be coming down with a sickness. This is stress.

How Does Stress Affect Your Daily Tasks?

There are many people, when faced with the above situation, who would just say "forget it!" and go back to bed. Others would get right to work, tackling every task on their to-do list. The problem is that neither one has the "go out and get 'em" attitude simply because:

1. They do not feel as well as they should be

2. They are not even out of bed yet and they already feel overwhelmed by the day's tasks

As you can see, what may seem like a routine Monday morning for a business owner can easily become the company's biggest downfall. Much of these troubles could be reduced through better organization skills and the outsourcing of some unprofitable tasks. However, even if you find that this is your routine Monday morning, you can face the day free from stress.

Stress can come in the following forms:

Acute Stress: This is short-term stress. It can either be positive stress (eustress) or it can be distress (what we typically think of when we hear the word "stress"). This is the kind of stress that we encounter in our everyday life. An example of this would be road rage.

Eustress: This type of stress is actually positive. It is what we experience during activities that are fun or exciting. It is what keeps us feeling alive.

Chronic Stress: This is the kind of stress that appears to be never-ending and impossible to escape. Examples of this type of stress include a taxing job or a terrible marriage.

Episodic Acute Stress: This is the type of stress that turns into a way of life. It simply runs rampant in your life. The result is a life filled with chaos.

Signs Of Chronic Stress

Chronic stress is by far the most vicious and negative forms of stress. This type of stress is what causes major complications and a number of physical symptoms, which include a suppressed immune system and chronic headaches. If left untreated, chronic stress can lead to:

- Obesity
- Hair loss
- Heart disease
- Depression
- Diabetes
- Hyperthyroidism
- Sexual dysfunction
- OCD (Obsessive Compulsive Disorder)
- Anxiety disorder
- Ulcers

Research shows that nearly ninety percent of doctor visits are for stress-related symptoms. Fortunately, the vast majority of stress in life can not only be managed, but eliminated altogether. The first step is to recognize stress and how it is affecting your life.

Start by asking yourself the questions below:

- At what times do you feel stressed?
- What kind of stress do you feel on a regular basis?
- How is stress affecting you on a physical, emotional and mental level?
- What types of things make you feel stressed?

Do you have issues with anger, anxiety or depression? These are deep rooted issues that can be improved and managed through the elimination of stress. Improving your general health may also help, but there may be other contributing causes that may require you to seek the help of an expert.

Steps To Take To Reduce And Eliminate Stress

Step One: Remove the cause of your stress, or at least reduce your exposure to it.

Take a look at your answers above. What moments cause you a great deal of stress? Can you eliminate any of these triggers?

For instance, if you feel stressed out by your customer support responsibilities, then the quickest way to get rid of this stress is to simply outsource the task. If lack of money to pay the bills is causing you stress, then you should consider working with a credit counselor or financial advisor to help you get your financial situation straightened out. This may not completely eliminate the stress, but it will provide you with a little more control. This will go a long way to reducing the amount of stress in your life.

Step Two: Pay attention to your thoughts. If you notice yourself thinking negative thoughts, start to replace them with positive ones. You can tackle this problem by making a list of negative thoughts that you have on a regular basis. Have the freedom to be honest with your list and try not to edit yourself. Jot down every little negative thought, which are typically just complaints, which comes to mind.

Common thoughts include:

- I am too busy for this.
- I will never be able to get this done.
- I am always so tired, angry and sick.
- I will never be able to take my business any further.

Examine these negative thoughts that you have and begin to turn them around. Transform them into positive affirmations. If you are finding yourself complaining about having no energy, turn that around and say, "I am always alert, awake and feeling alive." Whenever you notice yourself making a complaint or having a negative thought, stop what you are doing and say your affirmation out loud. There are many experts that recommend placing your affirmations in a place where you can see them. A great place would be the bathroom mirror. Once you have your affirmations posted, you can begin reciting them many times throughout the day. Eventually, those negative thoughts will disappear and you can begin removing other negative thoughts that you are experiencing.

Step Three: Take care of your health. Be sure that you get the proper amount of sleep each night. Exercise at least three times a week. Make changes to your diet so that you are eating more nutritious and health-promoting foods. These three things will be discussed in upcoming chapters. However, it is important to understand that exercise, sleep and diet play a crucial role in keeping your body and your mind in a better state to deal with stress. This means that even when you are feeling stressed, you can handle it with grace. In the end, this reduces the negative impact that stress will have on your body and your mental state.

Step Four: Consider taking supplements. There are many different natural supplements on the market that can help you cope with stress. St John's Wort is a great example. It is an herb that is frequently recommended for symptoms of depression.

Before you begin taking any kind of supplement you should first consult with your physician to see if they are right for you. There are some supplements, including St John's Wort, that are unable to be consumed with certain medications.

Step Five: Stress-reducing rituals. Develop a ritual for yourself that helps calm you down. Meditation is something that has helped many people maintain a relaxed and calm mind. Massages, bubble baths and aroma therapy can also work wonders to relax the mind and body.

Step Six: Practice gratitude. Take a look at your life and focus on the things that are good within it. Gratitude journals are a wonderful tool to have. By making regular entries in them, you will improve your memories of all the good things in your life. When you have gratitude for all that you do have, many other problems begin to disappear or seem far less important. If you are not really keen on the idea of keeping a journal, you can try to think of five things that you are grateful for each night before bed. Alternatively, you can practice this same routine in the morning after you get up. If you like, you can turn this into a ritual of sorts. For instance, you may spend every morning outside on your patio drinking a cup of coffee and giving thanks for all that you are and all that you have.

There is no reason that you should have to live with stress. You absolutely do not need to suffer through the symptoms and the illnesses that it causes. Aside from taking steps towards managing stress and reaching towards optimum health, it is important to understand that your sleep patterns, exercise routine and diet plays a major role in how your body and your mind responds to stress. The better your health, the better you will be at managing stress. In the long run, this will make you a far happier and more productive person.

You Are What You Eat! Changing Your Diet for Improved Productivity

Instead of lecturing you about how important it is to eat a healthy diet, let's just start by asking you a few questions.

☐ 1. Do you frequently get sick?

☐ 2. Are you a few pounds overweight?

☐ 3. Is your energy level where you want or need it to be?

☐ 4. Do you find that you sleep well at night?

☐ 5. Do you frequently experience digestive problems?

☐ 6. Do you completely lose your focus midway through the day?

☐ 7. Do you feel good?

You can probably see where we are going with this. If you answered yes to questions 1, 2, 5 and/or 6 and no to questions 3, 4 and/or 7, then your diet could likely use some tweaking.

By providing your body with the nutrients, rest and exercise that it needs, it allows one to feel great mentally and physically all the time. You will find that you have all of the mental clarity and energy that you need to be more productive throughout your day. It will become much easier to accomplish both your personal and your business goals.

Instead of just telling you to go on a diet or tell you how or what to eat, we are just going to give you some guidelines on which foods or nutrients are essential for optimum health. These foods will also help you gain more energy and a better mental outlook on life.

Powerful Protein

Protein is what doctors consider the building block of life. It is what burns fat and keeps your metabolism going. If we fail to take in enough protein, we simply fizzle out. You can judge whether or not you are getting enough protein by your energy levels. If you find yourself consistently feeling fatigued or sick, you may be lacking in protein.

Complete proteins come from animal products like chicken and fish. This means that the protein contains all of the essential amino acids the body needs. Many fruits, vegetables and grains also contain protein including milk, eggs, avocados, apricots, rice, quinoa, dates, bananas, cherries, figs, beans and nuts.

It is recommended that you maintain a ratio of 40:30:30 carbohydrates to fat to protein. In addition, it is also recommended that you consume protein with every meal. This becomes especially important if you will be exercising regularly.

For instance, if you are eating an apple, which contains twenty grams of carbohydrates, you should combine your snack with either a handful of nuts or a few tablespoons of nut butter (like peanut butter). This will provide you with the protein and fat that your body needs. Vegetables and fruits provide the body with many different minerals, vitamins and antioxidants. Antioxidants are what help the body to fight off free radicals and prevents cells from breaking down. This breakdown is what doctors believe contributes to major health problems like macular degeneration, heart disease, cancer and diabetes.

Vegetables And Fruits Are Nature's Medicine

According to the food pyramid, you should be consuming approximately five cups of fruits and vegetables each day. The best way to accomplish this is to make vegetables and fruits a part of every meal you eat. Sneak a handful of green vegetables into your morning omelet, eat a banana for a snack, add greens and a tomato to your sandwich, throw in a handful of berries in your yogurt and finally, add a big heaping serving of beans to your evening meal. As you can see, this example contains a variety of different fruits and vegetables. If you decide to eat an apple and four cups of spinach every day, you are missing out on a great deal of nutrients. Eat the foods that are in season and eat a variety of them every day.

Fats Are Not The Enemy

Fats have developed a bad reputation over the year. People just assume that the greater the amount of fat you consume, the fatter you become. The truth is that not all fats are bad and you actually *do* need to eat fat on a regular basis. Fats that are good for the body will help keep your brain and organs functioning properly. Overall, they lower the risk of disease. It should go without saying, however, that not all fats are created equal.

Here is what the Mayo Clinic offers on the topic of fats:

Good fats include:

- Polyunsaturated fats. These include vegetable oils like corn, safflower, soy, sunflower and cottonseed. Nuts and seeds also fall into this category.

- Monounsaturated fats. Peanut, olive and canola oils fit into this category. Avocados and certain nuts and seeds do as well.

- Omega-3 fatty acids. These come from cold water fish like mackerel, salmon and herring. This will also include walnuts, flaxseeds and flax oil.

Bad fats include:

- Trans fat from partially hydrogenated vegetable oils. These are commonly found in commercially processed baked goods including cookies, crackers and cake. They are also used for fried foods. Margarine and shortening also fall into this category.

- Saturated fats. This can come from animal products including red meats, poultry, eggs, seafood, cheese, butter and lard. Palm, coconut and other tropical oils are also considered saturated fats.

- Dietary cholesterol. These are found in animal products like eggs, dairy, butter, lard, poultry, seafood and red meats.

When shopping in the supermarket, make sure that you read the labels of the foods you are buying to see which types of fats they include. Stick with proteins that are lean like turkey, fish and chicken. Avoid consuming high levels of saturated fats and dietary cholesterol.

Let's take a moment to talk about fiber.

Fiber Does More Than Just Promote Regularity

The Harvard School of Public Health states that fiber is a certain type of carbohydrate which the body simply cannot digest. Adult women should aim for twenty grams of fiber each day. Men should aim for more than thirty grams. Fruits, vegetables, whole grain breads, beans and many breakfast cereals provide adequate amounts of fiber. Soluble fiber will partially dissolve in water. Insoluble fiber, on the other hand, will not. There are some key differences in these two different types of fiber and their effect on your risk of developing disease.

Now that we have gone over the ingredients that help to make up a healthy diet, we need to discuss what foods should be left out of your diet. These foods include:

- Sugar and high fructose corn syrup (sometimes labeled as corn syrup)
- Dietary cholesterol
- Saturated fats
- Excessive amounts of alcohol
- White flour and processed flours – these are often found in baked goods
- Excessive amounts of caffeine

Tips On How To Eat A Balanced Diet

Unfortunately, when you are busy building up a business and enjoying your life, you tend to put your diet at the bottom of your list of priorities. Eating healthy can easily become a chore that is too time consuming and very overwhelming. The fact of the matter is that eating healthy can actually be far more convenient and definitely more cost-effective than just grabbing whatever you can get your hands on.

Take Small Steps: If your end goal is to give your diet a complete overhaul, then making a number of changes all at once may not be the best option. Instead, make small changes. For instance, if you are in the habit of drinking five sodas each day, try only drinking four each day for an entire week. The next week, cut back to three sodas each day. Keep going until you reach the point where you are not drinking any soda at all.

Get In The Right Mindset: Remember that this is all about changing your lifestyle and your habits. This is not about making resolutions or any big proclamation.

Eat More Than Three Meals Each Day: For most people, consuming three meals each day is simply not enough to keep you going at full speed. Add exercise into the mix and you may have a real problem with energy levels. Most fitness gurus recommend consuming five to six small meals each day.

Make Plans: If you plan on cooking at home, go to the store each week with a shopping list already made. You can take this one step further by planning out your meals for the week so that you know exactly what you need to make your meals quickly and easily. There are many recipe websites out there that can help you prepare healthy meals in less than twenty minutes.

Indulge A Little: Every person has a favorite food. Do not deprive yourself of this food. If you absolutely love cookies, then eat cookies. Just be mindful of how many cookies you eat. There is no reason to eat the entire box in one sitting. When you deprive yourself of the foods you love, you begin to feel restrained. At one point or another, you are likely to go on an eating binge or give up on your changes altogether. Eat the foods you like and drink the drinks you like, but do so in moderation.

Mindful Eating: Be aware of the foods that you are putting into your body. This goes beyond just knowing what foods you are consuming, but also know what those foods provide to both your body and your health. Be aware of where your food is coming from and give thanks for the food that you are eating. Have gratitude for the nutrients that these foods provide.

Journaling: Start and maintain a food journal. More often than not, we are just simply unaware of the foods that we are putting into our bodies. We may think that we are eating a healthy diet, but in actuality, we are headed in the wrong direction. Food journaling is an excellent way to help you honestly and accurately assess your personal eating habits. Make the effort to write down each and every thing that you eat for a few weeks.

As you create your journal, make sure that you do not make any changes to your regular habits. Just act as you normally do. Once you are done with your journal, you can sit down and take a look at what you are eating and where you can make improvements. It may also be useful to make notes of when you were feeling the most energetic and focused.

Always Eat Breakfast: What your mother told you was correct; breakfast is by far the most important meal of the day. Start the day right by consuming a nutritious breakfast that is high in protein.

In order to determine what areas of your diet could use some improvement, answer the following questions.

- What negative eating habits do you already know need to be changed?
- What are your goals nutrition-wise?
- What are your current eating habits?
- How do you plan on improving your eating habits?

Remember that supplying your body with the nutrition that it needs will help you focus better, maintain higher energy levels and provide you with the stamina you need to run a business and enjoy all that life has to offer. Who wants to live a life where you spend your entire day working and then have no energy left to play with your family and friends?

Consuming the right foods will allow you to:

- Maintain high energy levels that will allow you to make it through the day with a smile on your face.
- Keep a positive outlook on life
- Find mental clarity, which is essential for all business responsibilities and tasks
- Enjoy a better night's sleep
- Remain free of illness
- Maintain a weight that is healthy
- Keep your hair, skin and teeth looking healthy
- Better manage stress
- Feel great both physically and mentally
- Provide you with better self-esteem
- Reach your goals

If you want to attain any of the above goals, you need to start making healthy changes to your lifestyle today. Remember to start out by making small changes and make sure that those changes are ones that promote a life filled with success, health and happiness.

How Exercise Can Help You Build a Better Business

Staying active through exercise is not only great for your physical health, but it also provides a number of mental health benefits as well. For example:

- Regular exercise helps you to sleep better.

- Being physically active releases endorphins. These are feel good hormones that are essential to a happy mind. They allow you to feel calm and content.

- Exercise helps the body and the mind to cope with stress. It also helps to regulate the body's hormones and its metabolism as well.

- Exercise is one of the best ways to improve your energy levels. When you first begin your exercise routine, you may feel fatigued. However, after a few weeks of regular activity, you will find that you wake up in the morning with more energy and it will last throughout the entire day.

How can exercise do all of these things? When you are physically active, your heart pumps faster. This increases the amount of oxygen that the body receives. It also releases endorphins. Even if you are feeling physically tired, the rush of endorphins can help keep you alert mentally. The amount of exercise that you do, the type of exercise you choose to engage in and your current shape will determine how much more alert your mind will become. Over time, exercise lowers the amount of body fat you carry around and also increases muscle mass. This makes your body far more efficient and energetic.

If all of these excellent mental health benefits are still not enough to get you up off of the couch or your desk, then take a peek at the health benefits listed below:

- Men's Health states that regular exercise has a number of positive health benefits. Many of these benefits are related to the heart. Rigorous activity can help strengthen your heart overall and make it a more efficient, larger muscle. Moderate amounts of exercise can improve your LDL cholesterol levels as well (this is the good cholesterol). It can also help improve the circulatory system, reduce blood fats and lower your blood pressure. All of these things help to reduce one's overall risk for heart disease, stroke and heart attack.

- According to The American Heart Association, nearly 250,000 deaths in the United States each year can be contributed to lack of exercise. That is nearly twelve percent of the total deaths each year.

- Exercise can also offer a number of other benefits, including improved flexibility, strengthened muscles and stronger bones. For women, this means a reduced risk for osteoporosis as well.

The Three Basic Types Of Exercise:

Strengthening: Strength training exercises include lifting weights, yoga, rock climbing, resistance training and Pilates. Strengthening exercises will help you maintain proper bone density, which can help prevent hip fractures later in life. This type of exercise will also help you maintain muscle tone and strength as you age. For those who are looking to lose

weight, muscle helps increase the amount of fat the body burns and improves your metabolism.

Flexibility: This type of exercise includes yoga, Pilates and resistance training. Many flexibility excrcises are also strengthening exercises as well.

Cardiovascular: More often than not, cardio is what people picture when they hear the word "exercise". This is also what sends most people back to bed or back onto the couch. Aerobics and running are the two most common forms of cardiovascular exercise. These are not the only two, however. Ice skating, bicycling, snowboarding, roller skating, skiing, dancing, swimming and walking are all great ways to get a good cardio workout. To put it simply, cardio just means that you are working your heart and your lungs.

What Type Of Exercise Is Best? How Often Should You Be Exercising?

Fitness experts and physicians often recommend exercising for thirty minutes every day. In an ideal situation, you would include a mixture of flexibility, strength training and cardio exercises in each session. Each person will have their own preferences. There are many people who prefer to engage in strength training or flexibility exercises instead of cardio. Others just love the simplicity of going out for a run each day. So, which is the right answer? The best thing that you can do is find exercises that you enjoy doing and ones that suits your personality. If you hate cardio workouts, then try walking for a half hour three times each week. You can then balance this out by doing yoga, Pilates or strength training on the days that you are not walking.

The key here is to find the time to workout so that you can make exercise a priority in your life.

The first thing that you need to do is get up off of the couch and start trying out new exercises. Find ones that you enjoy doing.

Make a list of all of the activities that you enjoy doing. Do not think about whether or not they could be considered exercise. If your body and your muscles are moving, then it can be considered exercise. Below are some options that you may not have considered.

- Lifting weights
- Swimming
- Aerobics
- Running
- Yoga
- Walking
- Bicycling

Going beyond the basics, you may also enjoy:

- Tennis
- Dancing
- Skating
- Hiking
- Rock climbing
- Jumping rope
- Basketball
- Kickboxing
- Soccer
- Baseball
- Skiing
- Snowboarding

If the activity is something that gets you up off of the couch and working your muscles, heart and lungs, then it *is* exercise. So, the first thing you should do is find exercise that you truly enjoy doing.

The second step is to actually make time for exercise. How you go about doing this will depend upon the type of person you are. If you are a very social person, you can join a club or a local league. This is a great way to get started. For instance, you can join a cycling club or the local soccer league.

If you are more of an introvert and the idea of joining a gym just does not suit your personality, then you can always consider purchasing a treadmill for your home. You can set it up right in front of the television if you like and exercise while watching your favorite shows. You can also go for walks, hike, jog, ride your bike or practice yoga. If you are a thrill seeker, you can try rock climbing, snowboarding or even mountain biking.

Take a minute to ask yourself the following questions about your exercise goals and habits:

- What kind of exercises do you enjoy?
- What kind of exercises do you currently do?
- What are some ways that you can include exercise into your daily routine?
- What are some ways that you can make your day more active? Could you walk to the store instead of driving there? Could you choose to take the stairs instead of the elevator?

When you can include regular exercise into your daily routine, you can:

- Maintain a weight that is healthy
- Sleep better at night
- Feel more attractive

- Maintain high energy levels
- Maintain a positive attitude
- Improve your overall physical appearance
- Improve your physical and mental well-being
- Reduce or eliminate illness
- Improve your confidence levels
- Achieve your goals

If you want to achieve any of these goals then you will need to start leading a healthier lifestyle. Begin by adding regular exercise to your routine so that you can enjoy a life that is healthier and happier.

Improve Sleep to Improve Your Productivity Levels

Have you ever heard someone say "I will sleep when I'm dead" or "Sleep is completely overrated"?

They may say this, but everyone knows that without sleep, they would be dead rather quickly.

The National Sleep Foundation found that nearly seventy million people in the United States alone have sleeping problems. Nearly forty million people in America suffer from some kind of chronic sleep disorder. In addition to this, between twenty and thirty million more have intermittent sleep problems.

It is estimated that sleep disorders and sleep deprivation cost Americans more than one hundred billion dollars each year in medical expenses, loss of productivity, sick leaves, environmental damage and property damage.

Those who suffer from the conditions listed below are also at a greater risk of developing a sleep disorder:

- Lack of exercise

- Diabetes

- Obesity

- Depression

- Poor dietary habits

- Improper use of prescription medications

The effects of sleep deprivation will typically depend upon the particular sleep disorder from which you are suffering. There are, however, some general side effects from lack of sleep. These include:

- Depression

- Blurred vision

- Quick weight loss or gain

- Dizziness

- Loss of memory

- High blood pressure

- Hallucinations

- Heart disease

- Nausea

- Irritability

- Tremors

- Inability to speak properly

A study that was reported by the Washington Post stated that nearly ten thousand adults in America between the ages of thirty-two and forty-nine and slept less than seven hours each night were at a greater risk of becoming obese.

This particular study was a part of a series of other studies whose results found a link between sleep disorders and other illnesses. For instance, the Nurses' Health Study found a link between irregular or insufficient sleep with greater risks of breast cancer, colon cancer, diabetes and heart disease. There are many other research groups throughout the country that have found many clues that may be able to explain why lack of proper sleep or sleep disruption has an effect on the roles that proteins and hormones play in these diseases.

There are physiologic studies that suggest sleep deprivation places the body into a high alert state. This increases the production of stress hormones and increases blood pressure. In turn, this increases your chance of developing heart disease or experiencing a stroke. In addition, people who are sleep deprived are likely to have higher levels of toxins in the blood, which increase inflammation. This has also proven to be a major contributor to stroke, heart disease, cancer and even diabetes.

What Does All Of This Information Mean?

What this means is good sleep is a critical part of maintaining optimum health. Without proper sleep, you put yourself at risk for a plethora of diseases and other mental health problems. Scientists are still unaware of all of the complications that come along with sleep deprivation and how it affects your overall health. They do know that sleep is far more important than most of us believe.

Sleep is critical. The body's circadian rhythm regulates just about everything including your diet, hormones and the body's cellular reproduction. These are crucial to maintaining organ and skin health. Remember that your cells make up your entire body.

What Are The Causes Of Poor Sleep?

You probably have some kind of idea of what causes your sleep issues if you have them. Some other causes may include:

- Obesity

- Lack of proper exercise

- Your diet choices

- Diabetes

- Poor sleeping habits

- Stress

- Certain medications

Fortunately, all of these causes can be reversed and your sleeping habits can be improved. Just about everyone experiences insomnia every once in awhile. However, you can take real steps towards improving your sleeping habits, which will reduce your stress levels, improve productivity and provide you with an abundance of energy.

How To Improve Your Sleeping Habits

As you now know, sleep is a crucial part of your productivity and health. For this reason, we have compiled a list of helpful tips to improve your sleep. However, if you are having real problems with chronic insomnia, you may need to see your physician or a sleep therapist as soon as possible.

- Eat a small snack. If you are exercising regularly, you may want to consider eating a small snack before you go to sleep. The key is to choose a snack that has fewer carbohydrates and higher levels of protein.

This combination will help the body to metabolize the meal while you are sleeping. When you wake up, you will feel far less hungry. You will also find it much easier to recover from your workouts.

- Get rid of the electronics. Remove the television, your telephone and your computer from your bedroom. The bedroom is a place to sleep and intimate moments – nothing else.

- Establish a nightly routine. This routine should be one that focuses on encouraging calmness. There are many people that choose to read for a half hour each night before bed. For example, you may have a protein bar at 8 PM while watching television. At 10 PM, you may brush your teeth, wash your face and take care of any other nightly bathroom rituals. Afterward, you climb into bed and read for a half hour before turning off your light at 10:30 PM, on the dot.

- Establish a morning routine. This starts by waking up at the same time each day. You can change your wake up time on the weekends if you truly wish. There are some people that abide by the natural sunrise clock, which gradually fills the room with light until it is time for you to wake up. The body's circadian rhythms naturally respond to light and dark.

- Go to bed at the same time each night and wake up at the same time each morning. Be sure that your bedroom is a place that is calming and peaceful. It should be free from distractions and other things that induce anxiety.

- Clear the slate before you go to sleep at night. It may be helpful to create a plan or a to-do list for the next day. This can really clear your mind and any negative thoughts you may be having. Once you have created your list, close your book and call it a night. Even if you have a lot to do the next day, you still need to let it all go before you sleep. If this kind of routine makes you feel a bit overwhelmed or stressed out before bed, then by all means, do not do it. Instead, try writing down five things that you are grateful for and try to sleep with a happy heart.

- In addition to all of this, it truly does help to sleep on a bed that is comfortable, to have pillows that allow you to sleep well and to wear clothing that is comfortable.

Now that we have discussed some ways to improve your sleep, let's take a look at some things you should avoid before going to bed.

- Do not drink caffeinated drinks six to seven hours before going to bed.

- Do not exercise two to three hours before going to bed.

- Do not drink more than one glass of wine before going to bed.

In order to improve your current sleeping habits, you will need to analyze your routine and any sleep related issues you may have. Start by asking yourself the questions below.

- Are you really getting the sleep that you need? When you wake up, do you feel alert, energized and focused throughout the entire day?

- What is your current sleep schedule?

- Can you develop a sleep ritual?

- How many hours of sleep do you want to aim for each night?

Finding a way to improve your sleeping habits will allow you to:

- Remain alert and focused throughout the day

- Maintain a healthier weight

- Experience mental clarity

- Remain healthy and free from disease

- Keep a positive outlook

- Better manage the stress in your life

- Improve your self-esteem

- Improve your physical appearance

- Help you to reach your goals

Begin making some healthy lifestyle changes today so that you can reach these goals listed above. Improving your sleep habits is a step in the right direction and will improve your overall health and happiness.

Finding Balance Is The Answer To A Successful Business

Working eighty or more hours per week and having millions of dollars in your bank account really is not much of a life.

Everyone has their own idea about what life is really means. Take some time to think about whether or not you are leading the life you really want.

Is your life filled with learning, laughter, joy, love, hobbies and your business?

What would you do if you suddenly had all of the time in the world and money was no object? Would you pick up a new skill? Would you find a new hobby or maybe spend more time on a hobby that you already love? Or, would you spend that time traveling around the world? What would you do?

If you do not make the time to enjoy the life that you create, your work begins to suffer, your health suffers and your life becomes completely out of balance. Brian Tracy wrote an article where he discussed some findings from the psychologist Sidney Jourard. Jourard found that nearly eighty-five percent of the happiness you experience in life will be a result of your personal relationships. The time you spend with the people you care about will be your primary source of joy and satisfaction in life. Accomplishments make up the other fifteen percent of your happiness.

What are you doing in the present moment to improve your personal relationships?

Leading a life that is balanced is something that is relative to each person, their personality, their goals in life and their lifestyle. It is important to not let other people determine whether or not you are leading a life that is balanced. Only you can know what is right for you. If you are happy in life and you make time for the things that you enjoy doing, then you are on the right track.

However, if you are feeling:

- Overwhelmed

- Angry

- Depressed

- Irritated

- Stressed

- Bored

- Lonely

- Have a negative outlook on life

There is a good chance that your life is out of balance. Let's take a close look at some ways that you can bring your life back into balance and maintain that balance.

1. What do you want to have more of in your life? What is it that you are missing? What are some things that you really want to do, but you are simply not making any time for those things? This can be anything you want it to be. It can be as simple as walking your dog more often, or it can be as complex as traveling the world.

2. What is keeping you from leading a balanced life? What challenges and obstacles stand in your way of reaching your goals listed above?

3. Develop a plan to overcome those obstacles. There are some obstacles that may be budget-related. Others may be issues with time and yet others may be personal obstacles. Devise a plan that will help you to overcome whatever obstacle you may have encountered.

How are you going to overcome your personal obstacles and find the time to really focus on the other things in your life? These are the things that provide you with laughter, with joy, with fun and help make up a balanced life.

Begin by creating your plan today. Start with an outline of what you want to do and then create a plan on how you are going to make this happen.

When you incorporate love, laughter, joy and fun into your life, you cultivate balance and also:

- Have a greater passion for your business

- Find joy in even the most humdrum of tasks

- Achieve a long-lasting state of mental clarity that is essential for carrying out daily tasks

- Remove clutter from your mind and negative thoughts

- Improve your energy levels

- Reduce your vulnerability to illness

- Maintain a healthy weight

- Manage stress with ease

- Feel better mentally and physically

- Improve confidence

- Achieve your goals

- Make your life feel more purposeful and fulfilling

- Live a longer life

If you really want to attain the things listed above, you need to pull yourself away from work and your desk on a regular basis. Make sure to take days off. Take weeks off if you can. Find a way to truly embrace and enjoy the things around you. Make time for family, friends and love. Make time to be creative, to learn and to take care of yourself.